LAST TRAIN TO HEAVEN

POEMS BY:

DAVE CROCKETT

The Last Train To Heaven

Copyright ©2023 by Dave Crockett
All rights reserved, including the right to reproduce this book or portions thereof in any form.

Designed by ThemeScape Digital Design and Chrissie Tomlinson
Printed in the United States of America

ABOUT THE AUTHOR.

Dave and his wife, Becky, have been members of First Baptist Church in Perry, Georgia for over 50 years. Dave is an ordained Deacon and has taught Sunday School for several years. Becky has taught Sunday School for over 40 years and has served on various church committees. Both Dave and Becky are retired educators. Through the years, Dave has jotted down poetic inspirations the Lord has given him. Dave and Becky are the proud parents of daughter Tracy, and sons Tony and Josh. Grandchildren Anna and Jase also bless their lives.

The Last Train To Heaven

The Last Train To Heaven

CONTENTS

BABY JESUS	*7*
HE IS THE ONE	*8*
DEMON MAN	*9*
WHEN IT'S OVER	*10*
HE IS NOT HERE	*11*
GOD CREATED	*12*
HE CARES	*13*
OUR ADVERSARY	*14*
HE IS ALWAYS CLOSE	*15*
MY WAY	*16*
HE IS THE WAY	*17*
WHAT'S THE REASON	*18*
I'M BUSY	*19*
GREATEST FRIEND	*20*
IN THANKSGIVING	*21*
FAITH	*22*
IN THE GARDEN	*23*
LIFE'S STORMS	*24*
IT IS I	*25*
THE TREE	*26*
LAST TRAIN TO HEAVEN	*27*
LORD OF LORDS	*28*
MAN	*29*
NEWS OF A SAVIOR	*30*
REMEMBER	*31*
DEPEND ON ME	*32*
SADDENED FACES	*33*

WHERE CAN YOU GO?	**34**
THE BOOK	**35**
LIFE	**36**
THE GALILEAN	**37**
FRIEND OF MINE	**38**
THE OLD MAN	**39**
WORLDLY TROUBLES	**40**
BROTHERS OF MINE	**41**
THE STRANGER	**42**
READ THE BOOK	**43**
THE WOMEN CAME	**44**
HEAR MY PLEA	**45**
THEY CAME	**46**
THIS GOD OF OURS	**47**
THOUGHTS FROM A DEER STAND	**48**

BABY JESUS

He was born just a little baby, tiny and small,
But He grew up to be King over us all.
He walked the hot, dry desert to bring peace and love,
As He came with a message from our Father above.
Despised and rejected, He carried on,
Trying to save us and lead us home.
Talking to multitudes, He spoke soft and low,
Telling the people about salvation and things they should know.
For three short years, He walked the ground,
Preaching and healing in many a town.
But unbelievers cursed Him and soon without pity,
Tried and killed Him in that Jerusalem city.
The Man was gone, but His death proclaimed,
Salvation through Him could be sweetly gained.

HE IS THE ONE

A tree has no voice, but it speaks so loud,
As it lifts its branches up toward the clouds.
As if honoring One so great above,
One that showers down His heavenly love.
A tree has roots that run so deep,
Roots that feed and from harm does keep.
Just like Jesus holds us in His arms,
Protecting His children from all worldly harm.
Jesus is the One who will nurture and trim,
If, only like the tree, we would rely solely on Him.
Winter storms come and blot out the sun,
But only have faith for He's the One
That will supply all we need,
If we just take the time to plant a tiny seed.

DEMON MAN

In the bowels of the earth, lurks a demon man,
Trying hard to devise an alternate plan.
Salvation through Christ is for naught says he,
For the road to happiness is only through me.
Dressed in red with eyes of green,
In all the wrong places he thinks we should be seen.
A mighty battle rages each day,
And angry he gets when we kneel down to pray.
The demon man is hard to refuse,
And worldly tricks he is ready to use,
To keep us all from using the Sword,
And defeating him in the name of the Lord.

WHEN IT'S OVER

When our life on earth is over,
And it's all been said and done,
Did you do what you should.....the battle was it won?
Did you live your life in happiness and
Grace did you find?
Did you pray to God to save you,
Did you find your peace of mind?
Did you love your neighbor and help in every way,
Did you go the extra mile for Christ every day?

The Last Train To Heaven

HE IS NOT HERE

The women listened in amazement as they heard
the angel say,
"Go and tell the others that He is risen today."
Oh, what glorious news the women had to spread,
Jesus Christ, our Savior, had risen from the dead.
Many found it hard to believe like Thomas,
But we can always remember,
Jesus will keep His promise.

GOD CREATED

In the still, quiet void nothing moves about,
Suddenly, after millenniums of silence comes a great shout!
"Let there be light" and it was so.
God created the earth and saw it was good,
He brought forth life, the waters, and animal-hood.

God then made man in His own image and gave him a home,
A beautiful Eden in which he could roam.
The man was lonely and needed a mate,
But if only man knew what lurked in his fate.
God gave man a woman to share the graceful life,
To care for the garden as he cared for her as his wife.

Time passed pleasantly and goodness abound,
Man enjoyed the beauty that shone all around.
Alas, humanness soon played its part,
As deceit and trickery found the woman's heart.
A serpent, cunning and wise,
Crept into the garden and captured her eyes.

The woman listened and soon went astray,
Bringing on mankind the ills of today.
Man and woman were punished for their sin,
Never to enter the garden again.

Put forth into the world to work and sweat,
But the Creator of Life wasn't through yet.
He put forth His plan and gave man a way,
To enter into heaven at the end of his day.
Live in Jesus and do your best,
Believe in Christ, and He'll do the rest.

The Last Train To Heaven

HE CARES

It's hardly worth the living if you're living alone,
Even though friends surround you, and children fill
your home.
Do you have a longing for something you can't find,
Is there something missing that would give you
peace of mind?
Are worldly things binding you and keeping your
spirit down,
Do you face each day smiling or do your wear a frown?
Is it such a struggle to survive each day?
If so, listen to what I have to say.
There is a Counselor who'll bring your life sweet accord,
Who might this be you ask...it's Jesus Christ, the Lord.
You think your life is full and no help do you need,
Well, think a bit and of this do take heed.
There's One who cares and great love has shown,
It's hardly worth the living, if you are living alone.

OUR ADVERSARY

He moves about quietly ever so sly,
With a curl on his lip and a gleam in his eye.
He whispers softly and tells us its fine,
To do whatever that comes to our mind.
He breaks up homes and causes us great pain,
He sleeps in greed and Satan's his name.
All that is good is not his domain,
He likes to meddle and hear us complain.
He likes for children to question mom and dad,
He likes for faces to be long and sad.
Never let him control you and make you his own,
Fight him fiercely and leave him alone.
He's the devil by trade and his tail's his sword,
But we can defeat him with the help of the Lord.

The Last Train To Heaven

HE IS ALWAYS CLOSE

In this world of ours, trouble is all around.
People cheat and lie, and it's hard to hear above
the sound,
Of gnashing teeth and bitter talk as through this world
We attempt to walk.
But, Lord, as each day dawns, I know this to be true,
That when walls close in, and I come to need you,
I can just close my eyes, and I am ministered unto.
When I become weary and patience wears thin,
I simply close my eyes and you speak again.
Easing the loneliness and letting your peace flow in.
When doubts and fears toss us about,
And sorrows and burdens test us out,
I can rest assured you'll see us through,
Cause when I close my eyes I can always see you.

MY WAY

Life's struggle was hard and I did my best,
To battle the problems, cares, and all the rest.
I worked hard and tried to provide,
The necessities of life—but pride
Kept me saying—I can do it my way.
Through the years, time came and went,
And on self-reliance my course was bent.
Pressures mounted, but they heard me say,
I can do it my way.
The end time came and before Christ I stood,
Wanting to be part of His brotherhood.
Let me enter, Jesus, I pray,
"I'm sorry", He said, "You did it your way."

The Last Train To Heaven

HE IS THE WAY

He came out of Galilee with a smile on His face,
Full of love, peace, and saving grace.
He walked among men and healed their wounds,
He cared for children and brought men from their tombs.
He welcomed the young and cherished the old,
Tenderly loving each and every soul.
Yet, He was scorned and left to die,
As thousands shouted, crucify!
But down through the ages, He has given a way,
To be with Him in heaven—are you ready for Him today?

The Last Train To Heaven

WHAT'S THE REASON

Each day dawns, but what's the reason,
Just to exist and wait out the season?
Time is cruel and takes its toll,
Wearing down the body and wrinkling the soul.
Things I did and still wish to do,
Are gone forever leaving me blue.
Each day dawns, but what's the reason,
Just to exist and wait out the season?
Wouldn't it be best when these times appear,
To cease to worry and retreat from here?
Is the purpose to struggle and carry on,
Feeling worthless and striving alone?
Each day dawns, but what's the reason,
Just to exist and wait out the season?
What is the answer? Does it exist?
Or is it lost in some deep, dark abyss?
Maybe it's there waiting to be found,
But as I listen, I hear not a sound.
Each day dawns, but what's the reason,
Just to exist and wait out the season?

I'M BUSY

Hello, my son, how are you today?
Not now, Lord, I've got to be on my way.
Are you sure you want to go in that bar?
Not now, Lord, I've got to park my shiny new car.
But is that woman really your wife?
Not now, Lord, its just part of life.
Do you really have to drink to have some fun?
Not now, Lord, ain't she a pretty one?
How are your kids, are they at home?
Not now, Lord, there's more oats to be sown.
But how about your soul, has it been saved?
Not now, Lord, I'm not ready for the grave.
How is your business? Is it completed?
Not now, Lord, but some think I have cheated.
Been to church lately, its important you know?
Not now, Lord, my family will go.
Before you leave, Lord, just a question of you,
Where is everyone...suddenly I seem all alone?
Not now, son, I'm on my way home.

GREATEST FRIEND

When the world gets dark and angry,
And people put you down,
When despairing words are spoken,
And troubles are all around,
Let not your heart be troubled,
For there's One who can ease the pain,
Smooth those sharp words and chase away the rain.
He can move a mountain, or ease a fear so small,
His name is Jesus, the greatest friend of all.

IN THANKSGIVING

Though we live in strife and desolation,
With rendering hearts and in deprivation,
We have much to be thankful for.
Though nations growl and neighbors fuss,
And darkness seems too close on us,
We have much to be thankful for.

Oh, there are conditions surrounding us that
Depress and make us sad.
There too, are many reasons to be happy and glad.
We have much to be thankful for.
Health, love, and friends might top a list,
But above all, let's remember this,
We have much to be thankful for.
Greatest among these is our God and His loving Son
Whose unselfish death, salvation for us won.
We have much to be thankful for.

A nation that's strong and protects our rights,
A country that stands against tyranny's might.
We have much to be thankful for.
Churches that speak of the Savior's name,
Telling of how He shouldered our blame,
We have much to be thankful for.

So, during the season when things are good,
And celebration all around we see,
Remember Him is my solemn plea,
And let your voices soar, for He is Lord and that
Is much for us to be thankful for.

FAITH

Faith in Jesus can brighten your day,
You only need to open your heart and pray.
He will lead you in your daily trod,
But of the man who knows not God,
What of him we have cried?
In birth was he born, on earth did he live,
And without salvation he simply died.

IN THE GARDEN

In the cold, damp garden, He wept alone,
Knowing soon His time on earth would be gone.
As friends slept peaceably, and guarded Him not,
Roman soldiers were marching to this holy spot.

Arousing our Lord, they stood in place,
As Judas, His disciple, kissed His face.
Take Him away was the soldiers' cry,
As death on the cross for Jesus was nigh.

Taken before power no fault was found,
But no pardon was granted because of the sound
Of thousands demanding that Jesus die,
As they shouted loudly, crucify! Crucify!

The people were granted their sinful choice,
As Pilate could hardly ignore the people's voice.
Christ was sacrificed at the people's whim,
But little did they know—He died for them.

LIFE'S STORMS

When life is hard and full of storms,
Let us seek shelter in Jesus' arms.
When we have sinned and ventured afar,
Let us come home, Lord, where you are.
When we're weak and tempted by Satan's charm,
Take us and hold us and keep us from harm.
When our burdens grow heavy, and we seem alone,
Let us remember Calvary and the courage
you've shown.
When worldly things entrap us, and fame do we seek,
Let us grow humble and listen as you speak.
When our problems grow heavy and our face
hangs sad,
Let us remember the pain and agony you must
have had.
So, when the world is dark, and we need shelter from the
storms,
Let us remember you, Lord, and your waiting arms.

IT IS I

Oh, my soul thirsts for the answer,
As my mind searches the dark abyss.
For a leader—be it him or the other.
I can no longer live in a manner such as this.
Oh, the world is cold and unloving,
And man, my brother, keeps on shoving.
The piercing sounds of my tormented heart
Vibrates the night,
As I strive to conjure up the might,
To break away from hell's bondage.
A faint whisper begins from far away,
Straining, straining, I lean to listen
To what it will say.
A message filters through my conscious,
"Hear me, and pray."
Who brings this message so loud and clear?
Who comes this night and brings me cheer?
Who comes to soothe my human fear,
"It is I, said He. "I am Jesus."

The Last Train To Heaven

THE TREE

The mighty tree spreads its arms in adoring love,
As if praising the great God above.
Its strong stout trunk has stood the test of time,
As has Jesus, the great Savior of all mankind.
The tree has roots that penetrate the soil,
To help it survive winter's freeze and summer's boil.
Just like Jesus, who gives us life,
And power to withstand trouble and strife.

LAST TRAIN TO HEAVEN

We know the Lord is coming, we know He's coming soon.
You don't have to worry, for His train has lots of room.
But don't be left at the station, when the final whistle blows,
And you must live your life as God's Word clearly shows.
The Conductor's patiently waiting to help you on your way,
So don't waste your time, get a ticket without delay.
The train is filling fast, and the schedule is not yet complete,
But when the train starts its run, there won't be time to speak.
This train is a special one, running just one time,
So don't get caught in a long waiting line.
The engineer has his orders when the signal comes down,
To fire up the engines and cover lots of ground.
The train will depart the earth and head for a heavenly place,
Where all with a ticket, will be greeted by our Lord's smiling face.

LORD OF LORDS

He struggled along the dusty street
Beneath the heavy load.
Sometimes falling at the feet
Of those standing along the road.
Wearing only a girdle loin and a
Crown made of thorns,
But with courage, He struggled on
For this was why He was born.
Bone weary and aching, perhaps with thirst,
He continued on for He must compete
His dreaded mission first.
People scoffed and jeered as He passed them by,
On His way to the Skull Hill where shortly He would die.
No mercy was shown Him as He was nailed to a tree,
Raised up high He was so everyone could see.
The Man grimaced in pain and water did he need,
But the Spirit was willing to carry out the deed.
Darkness fell around the hill, and everyone was afraid,
But no one realized the debt was now being paid.
As life left the Man and darkness quieted things,
People now realized this was truly the Lord of Lords
And the King of Kings.

The Last Train To Heaven

MAN

From the dawn of time man has been
Cruel, heartless, and full of sin.
Cheat your neighbor not once, but twice,
Don't dare mention the name of Christ.
Go your way....run your race,
Don't stop to see the pain
On your neighbor's face.
Hurry, hurry, don't delay,
There's no need for prayer today.
We're in the world to push and shove,
Who needs faith, eternity or love?
Oh, that was yesterday and now we see,
A man, broken and lost, without one plea.
Tears streaming, he's on bended knee,
Saying, but Lord, why can't you take me?

NEWS OF A SAVIOR

Since the dawn of time, man has had a yearn,
For news of a Savior, he has wanted to learn.
The Word came on a night cool and clear,
As shepherds were told of a child so dear.
The Savior was born on this glorious day,
Wrapped in swaddling clothes on clean, yellow hay.
Up He grew, bold and strong,
Teaching everyone right from wrong.
Men were puzzled by this gentle King,
For deliverance from bondage was He to bring.
But fighting and death was not His plan,
For He only taught love for our fellow man.
People were healed and saved from sin,
But these miracles were lost in the din
Of the ones crying—crucify Him!
The crowd gathered behind the tall iron gate,
Waiting to hear of Jesus' fate.
"I find no fault," cried Pilate, the man,
Who could have saved Him with a wave of his hand.
But the plan was laid and orders read,
Put the Christ in chains and soon shall He be dead.
Up the hill, Christ carried His heavy load,
Sometimes stumbling on the rocky road.
The hour came and on this day,
Nails were hammered as our Lord lay.
The sky darkened and thunder roared,
As life ebbed from Jesus, our Lord.
People standing near surely heard,
Our Lord give the final word.
"It is finished," they heard Him cry,
Then for your soul and mine, our Savior would die.
But be not saddened and cast down,
For Jesus did not remain buried in the ground.
Up He arose and walked among men,
Guaranteeing us freedom from ages of sin.

REMEMBER

When storm clouds gather around us,
And sharp tongues cut us deep,
When surface friends befail us,
And troubles grow mountain steep,
Let not our hearts and spirits sink.
But let us all remember as we pause and think,
There is One who can help us and
Jesus is His name.
He's the One who died for us,
And took all the blame.
So, when times get hard and no light can we see,
Just remember Jesus, the One who died on Calvary.

DEPEND ON ME

You can always depend on me,
I won't ever let you down.
Even when no light you can see,
Or when trouble is all around.

You can always lean on me,
When things are going bad.
You can always count on me,
Even when times are hard and sad.

You can put your faith in me,
I'll never let you down.
In me, joy and peace can be found.
Don't be afraid to believe in me,
Even though my face you cannot see.

On Him, you can count, lean and depend,
The feeling of love, peace, and hope never end.
Take my hand and suffer no further,
Who am I, I am the Lord—your Father.

SADDENED FACES

Here I stand on this busy street,
Watching the people on hurrying feet.
With saddened faces they pass me by,
Not smiling at all—I know not why.
Not stopping to speak they hurry on,
As if afraid, they'll be left alone.
With skin drawn tight, their faces stare,
I wonder if they know I really care?
My heart yearns to tell of one great love,
That showers down from heaven above.
They need only to ask—once not twice,
And they will receive it from Jesus Christ.

WHERE CAN YOU GO?

When your load is heavy with the burdens of the world,
Where can you go, but to the Lord?
When friends forsake you, and put you down,
Where can you go, but to the Lord?
When doubt and fear fill your days,
Where can you go, but to the Lord?
When your home life becomes strained and worn,
Where can you go, but to the Lord?
When making a living becomes a ton of bricks,
Where can you go, but to the Lord?
When storm clouds rain on your best laid plans,
Where can you go, but to the Lord?
When quiet death comes, and you've been saved,
Where can you go, but to the Lord?

THE BOOK

Troubled and worn, I could not find,
The path to joy, and peace of mind.
One day while wandering, I stumbled upon,
A decaying old cross, lying all alone.
Curiously, I knelt to take a look,
And found beneath, a worn out book.
With trembling hands, I opened and read,
How a man called Jesus had died, yes bled,
To save the world from all its sin,
Then I placed it underneath again.
For now I knew where I could find,
That lost joy and peace of mind.
With a glow in my heart, I walked away,
Hoping some other lost soul would pass by here today.

LIFE

The pain of life burns deep in the soul,
It turns the young into the ravaged old.

Where love once thrived, strong and bold,
Now lives a heart turned hard and cold.

The excitement is gone from the sparkling eyes,
Replaced by the bitter drops from the sobs and sighs.

The attraction of youth has wrinkled and gone,
Leaving behind one sad and alone.

The mind questions and does not understand,
What happened to the smiles and the touch of the hand.

Subtle it came and took root and grew,
Weakening a bond shared by an unaware two.

This pain of life brings trouble and despair,
It creates doubt and brings sorrow to bear.

The pain of life as the story is told,
Kills the heart and burns up the soul.

THE GALILEAN

Through life's troubles do not despair,
For there is someone just waiting to care.
Though times are hard and words get sharp,
Listen intently for that golden harp.
Alone, life's burdens are heavy to bear,
Simply, let the Galilean shoulder a share.
He came to earth and triumphed in spite,
Of a friend's betrayal and Caesar's might.
He gave His all, don't you see,
For poor, wretched sinners like you and me.

FRIEND OF MINE

Is your heart heavy laden,
Is the world dark and cold?
Is the world too much with you,
Has the devil got your soul?
Do you struggle through life without even a smile?
If this is the case, your life isn't worthwhile.
Our burdens are many, and our cares seem like lead,
But someone has told me, or is it something I've read?
That there's One who loves us, and gives life a shining gloss,
Yet, He once died on a cruel, wooden cross.
This One is Jesus, a close friend of mine,
Just open your heart and give Him a little time.
He'll cleanse your wounds and remove all snares,
For He so loves the world, and He really, really cares.

THE OLD MAN

The old man lived alone in a rambling shack,
Owning nothing at all but the clothes on his back.
Yet, he was rich not in silver or gold,
But in knowing that Jesus had saved his soul.
Times had been hard throughout his life,
He had lost his farm and fever took his wife.
Yet, through the problems, he stood firm and tall,
Letting his Lord share the load, troubles and all.

WORLDLY TROUBLES

My heart weighs heavy with the burdens of the world,
Everywhere I turn, there's only trouble and woe.
You can see them in my eyes and through the wrinkles they show.
Decisions to make and jobs to complete,
Everyday I seem to go down in defeat.
People are cruel and have no time to spare,
They are all prosperous, why should they care?
Times goes by slowly when you're beaten down,
It seems not to matter that you're even around.
Is there an answer to all of this?
Is there a way to hope and happiness?
I remember long ago in a book it did read,
Knock and the door shall open, ask, and you shall receive.
Is this true...can it be?
Let me find that book...I think I'll see.

BROTHERS OF MINE

Where are we going brothers of mine,
Are we helping, sharing, to others are we kind?
Are we content to live each of God's precious days,
Searching, groping, stumbling in a haze?
People are hungry, sick and depressed,
How say you could we help them the best?
Give them clothing, shelter, and pat on the back
you say,
Why not fall on our knees and teach them to pray.

THE STRANGER

Oh, the way was weary as I struggled on without purpose, without a home,
In tattered clothing and a face forlorn, I shuffled along wondering why I was born.
Hungry and tired with aching feet, I stopped in a shade to escape the heat.
Lying in the cool of the spreading oak, tears from my eyes rolled down my throat.
Sighing heavily I struggled to find a reason to continue in this state of mind.
Talking out loud, I called to the wind, why shouldn't to my life, I put an end?
"For many reasons," a voice called back—many things are wrong, but it's faith you lack."
Looking up slowly, I saw a face that glowed with love and apparent grace,
A strange looking man dressed in purest white, stood over me with a smile so slight.
Where did he come from this man so fair, dressed in robe with long flowing hair?
We talked for a while and then he was gone, yet, strangely, I knew I wasn't alone.
The sun seemed brighter, and the grass was green, the flowers were the prettiest I have ever seen.
New hope in life now ran through me as the face of the stranger gave peace, hope, and love to me.
Let me go on my way and seek to find, people who have doubt and fears like mine.
Let me help them, and show them love just like the stranger that appeared from above.

READ THE BOOK

Is your heart heavy and full of sin,
Do you need love and the warmth of a friend?
Has the world caught up with you and burdened you down,
Are trouble and pain the only sounds you hear?
Is your way dark and spent without cheer?
If so, my friend, take this advice,
Open the Bible and read, yes twice,
About how your life can change through the grace of Jesus Christ.

THE WOMEN CAME

The women came with saddened faces to the place where Jesus lay,
But were astonished when no traces of Him were found this day.
Why have they done this, and where have they gone,
The ones who have stolen Him, and rolled away the stone?
Faces showed of worry, and flesh shook with fright,
But all doubts were washed away with the glow of angel light.
Fear not ye were the spoken words that soothed the women's fear,
I know ye seek Jesus, but know that He's not here.
For our Lord has risen, surely as He said,
Go and tell the others, He is not among the dead.
The women departed quickly and left without delay,
For news of the resurrection, they had to share today.
Though some were doubtful and proof they had to see,
I'll never doubt that Jesus died and rose for you and me.

The Last Train To Heaven

HEAR MY PLEA

Hear my plea, Lord, and walk with me,
Through this world of sin and misery.
Hear my plea, Lord, and talk with me,
Let me listen and know more about thee.
Hear my plea, Lord, and sing with me,
Songs of joy and divine ecstasy.
Hear my plea, Lord, and comfort me,
Though the dark clouds of sin around us be.
Hear my plea, Lord, and strengthen me,
To speak of your salvation that sets us free.

THEY CAME

The morning was chilling and the dew was on the ground,
As we were awakened from sleep by the sound,
Of military metal in the form of Roman sword,
As they came marching to take Jesus, our Lord.
How would they know Him, this one they did seek?
This was soon settled by a kiss on the cheek.
By Judas, a friend whose heart had turned cold,
At the sight and sound of tantalizing gold.
The chill of fright soon fled from my bones,
As Jesus was led down the road of stones.
My soul cried out—go stand in the way,
They shall not harm Him, I was heard to say.
Gathering up courage, my hand gripped the knife
That wanted to free Jesus and save Him His life.
Charging forward bright metal did I see,
As a soldier rammed home a sword into me.
Life left my body as my eyes found His face,
And I knew from the smile, He gave me His grace.
A startling sound then rang in my ears,
As I awakened with eyes full of tears.
Knowing full well it was all just a dream.
Rising from bed, wiping away the sweat,
I knew He had died and without regret.
For my soul and yours, He suffered the pain,
Hung on the cross and shouldered our blame.

THIS GOD OF OURS

Where did He come from, this God of ours,
The One who makes the wind, and brings us flowers?
When did He begin and how did He plan,
To create the world and place on it, man?
How did He know man would not be still,
How did He know we would rob, lie and kill?
Why does He prolong the world in its mess?
The answer to this, we don't have to guess.
For God had planned that by and by,
His Son would come and for us, He would die.

THOUGHTS FROM A DEER STAND

The world is too much with us at times,
Shaking our faith and worrying our minds.
Troubles are all around and tragedy we see,
But the world ain't ugly, looking down from a tree.

Though our lives were changed forever back on nine one-one,
The assurance of God's dominion comes up with the rising Sun.
Our high rise monuments came down for all the world to see,
But the world ain't ugly, looking down from a tree.

From up high you see the leaves of red, yellow, orange, and gold,
That color the trees that stand so tall and bold.
Man's evil has appeared and causes concern for you and me,
But the world ain't ugly, looking down from a tree.

The animals scurry along crossing the old logging road,
Unaware that in lands far away, the deadly
bombs explode.
People are dying so that we can remain free,
But the world ain't ugly, looking down from a tree.

Hopefully, one day the world will be at peace,
As all the fighting and hostilities cease.
Again we can laugh and be carefree,
Knowing the world ain't ugly, looking down from a tree.

The Last Train To Heaven

Made in the USA
Columbia, SC
23 November 2024